Alfred's INSTRUMENTAL PLAY-ALONG

Pop & Rock Hits
INSTRUMENTAL SOLOS

CONTENTS

D1560470

Arranged by Bill Galliford, Ethan Neuburg and Tod Edmondson

© 2011 Alfred Music Publishing Co., Inc.
All Rights Reserved. Printed in USA.

ISBN-10: 0-7390-8011-3
ISBN-13: 978-0-7390-8011-5

Alfred

ANIMAL

Words and Music by
TIM PAGNOTTA, TYLER GLENN,
BRANDEN CAMPBELL, ELAINE DOTY
and CHRISTOPHER ALLEN

Animal - 8 - 1

4

Animal - 8 - 4

6

8

84 *Chorus:*

IN MY HEAD

Words and Music by
CLAUDE KELLY, JONATHAN ROTEM
and JASON DESROULEAUX

Moderate pop rock (♩ = 112)

In My Head - 6 - 1

12

21 GUNS

Words and Music by
BILLIE JOE, GREEN DAY,
DAVID BOWIE and JOHN PHILLIPS

21 Guns - 5 - 1

21 Guns - 5 - 2

18

21 Guns - 5 - 3

20

21 Guns - 5 - 5

FIREWORK

Words and Music by
KATY PERRY, MIKKEL ERIKSEN,
TOR ERIK HERMANSEN, SANDY WILHELM
and ESTER DEAN

Moderate rock ($\quarternote$ = 126)

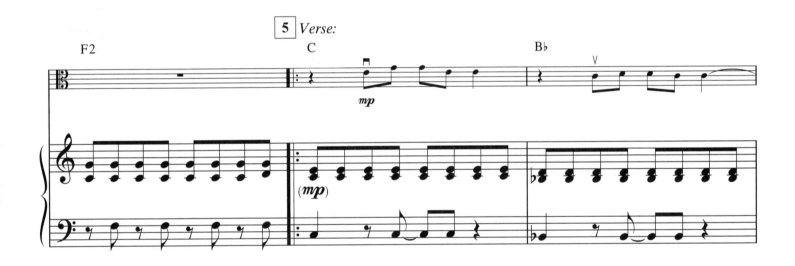

Firework - 7 - 1

22

Firework - 7 - 7

BOULEVARD OF BROKEN DREAMS

Words by
BILLIE JOE

Music by
GREEN DAY

Boulevard of Broken Dreams - 4 - 3

GRENADE

Words and Music by
CLAUDE KELLY, PETER HERNANDEZ,
BRODY BROWN, PHILIP LAWRENCE,
ARI LEVINE and ANDREW WYATT

Grenade - 5 - 1

Alfred's
INSTRUMENTAL
PLAY-ALONG

Pop & Rock Hits
INSTRUMENTAL SOLOS

CONTENTS

Arranged by Bill Galliford, Ethan Neuburg and Tod Edmondson

© 2011 Alfred Music Publishing Co., Inc.
All Rights Reserved. Printed in USA.

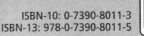

ISBN-10: 0-7390-8011-3
ISBN-13: 978-0-7390-8011-5

ANIMAL

Words and Music by
TIM PAGNOTTA, TYLER GLENN,
BRANDEN CAMPBELL, ELAINE DOTY
and CHRISTOPHER ALLEN

Animal - 3 - 1

4

84 Chorus:

98

3

IN MY HEAD

Words and Music by
CLAUDE KELLY, JONATHAN ROTEM
and JASON DESROULEAUX

In My Head - 3 - 1

6

21 GUNS

Words and Music by
BILLIE JOE, GREEN DAY,
DAVID BOWIE and JOHN PHILLIPS

21 Guns - 2 - 1

33 *Bridge:*

41 **45** *Chorus:*

Track 8: Demo
Track 9: Play Along

FIREWORK

Words and Music by
KATY PERRY, MIKKEL ERIKSEN,
TOR ERIK HERMANSEN, SANDY WILHELM
and ESTER DEAN

Moderate rock (♩ = 126)

Firework - 2 - 1

46 Bridge:

54 Chorus:

70

BOULEVARD OF BROKEN DREAMS

Track 10: Demo
Track 11: Play Along

Words by
BILLIE JOE

Music by
GREEN DAY

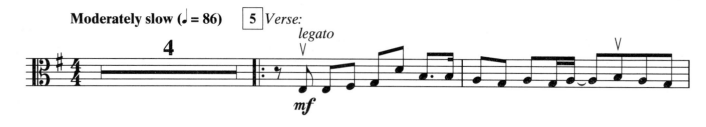

Boulevard of Broken Dreams - 2 - 1

Boulevard of Broken Dreams - 2 - 2

Track 12: Demo
Track 13: Play Along

GRENADE

Words and Music by
CLAUDE KELLY, PETER HERNANDEZ,
BRODY BROWN, PHILIP LAWRENCE,
ARI LEVINE and ANDREW WYATT

Grenade - 2 - 1

JUST THE WAY YOU ARE

Track 14: Demo
Track 15: Play Along

Words and Music by
KHALIL WALTON, PETER HERNANDEZ,
ARI LEVINE and KHARI CAIN

Just the Way You Are - 2 - 1

HAVEN'T MET YOU YET

Track 16: Demo
Track 17: Play Along

Words and Music by
MICHAEL BUBLÉ, ALAN CHANG
and AMY FOSTER

Haven't Met You Yet - 2 - 1

RHYTHM OF LOVE

Words and Music by
TIM LOPEZ

SMILE

Track 20: Demo
Track 21: Play Along

Words and Music by
MATTHEW SHAFER, BLAIR DALY,
J.T. HARDING and JEREMY BOSE

Smile - 2 - 1

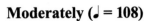
Track 22: Demo
Track 23: Play Along

NEED YOU NOW

Words and Music by
DAVE HAYWOOD, CHARLES KELLEY,
HILLARY SCOTT and JOSH KEAR

Moderately (♩ = 108)

Need You Now - 2 - 1

INSTRUMENTAL SOLOS

This instrumental series contains themes from Blizzard Entertainment's popular massively multiplayer online role-playing game and includes 4 pages of art from the World of Warcraft universe. The compatible arrangements are carefully edited for the Level 2-3 player, and include an accompaniment CD which features a demo track and play-along track. Titles: Lion's Pride • The Shaping of the World • Pig and Whistle • Slaughtered Lamb • Invincible • A Call to Arms • Gates of the Black Temple • Salty Sailor • Wrath of the Lich King • Garden of Life.

(00-36626) I Flute Book & CD I $12.99

(00-36629) I Clarinet Book & CD I $12.99

(00-36632) I Alto Sax Book & CD I $12.99

(00-36635) I Tenor Sax Book & CD I $12.99

(00-36638) I Trumpet Book & CD I $12.99

(00-36641) I Horn in F Book & CD I $12.99

(00-36644) I Trombone Book & CD I $12.99

(00-36647) I Piano Acc. Book & CD I $14.99

(00-36650) I Violin Book & CD I $16.99

(00-36653) I Viola Book & CD I $16.99

(00-36656) I Cello Book & CD I $16.99

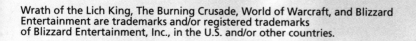

LICENSED BLIZZARD ENTERTAINMENT PRODUCT

Rolling Stone®

INSTRUMENTAL SOLOS · VOLUME 1 & VOLUME 2

Rolling Stone® Magazine's "The 500 Greatest Songs of All Time" is the ultimate celebration of the greatest rock & roll songs of all time. The editors of *Rolling Stone®* called on a five-star jury of singers, musicians, producers, industry figures, critics and, of course, songwriters. The 172 voters, who included Brian Wilson, Joni Mitchell and Wilco's Jeff Tweedy, nominated 2,103 songs in virtually every pop-music genre of the past half-century and beyond, from Hank Williams to OutKast. The results were tabulated according to a weighted point system. Alfred is proud to introduce an impressive new instrumental play-along collections that make songs from the *Rolling Stone 500* playable to music makers everywhere!

Selections from *Rolling Stone®* Magazine's 500 Greatest Songs of All Time: Instrumental Solos, Vol. 1 & 2

Each book contains a carefully edited part that is appropriate for Level 2-3 players, and a fully orchestrated accompaniment CD that includes both demo and play-along tracks for each song. Vol. 1 titles: Both Sides, Now • Desperado • Everyday People • A Hard Day's Night • Honky Tonk Women • Moondance • (We're Gonna) Rock Around the Clock • Soul Man • When a Man Loves a Woman • and more. Vol. 2 titles: Blueberry Hill • Dancing Queen • Hotel California • How Deep Is Your Love • I Got You (I Feel Good) • In the Midnight Hour • (I Can't Get No) Satisfaction • Spirit in the Sky • You Send Me • and more.

VOL. 1	VOL. 2		
(00-30335)	(00-30842)	Flute (Book & CD)	$12.95
(00-30338)	(00-30845)	Clarinet (Book & CD)	$12.95
(00-30341)	(00-30848)	Alto Sax (Book & CD)	$12.95
(00-30344)	(00-30851)	Tenor Sax (Book & CD)	$12.95
(00-30347)	(00-30854)	Trumpet (Book & CD)	$12.95
(00-30350)	(00-30857)	Horn in F (Book & CD)	$12.95
(00-30353)	(00-30860)	Trombone (Book & CD)	$12.95
(00-30359)	(00-30866)	Violin (Book & CD)	$14.95
(00-30362)	(00-30869)	Viola (Book & CD)	$14.95
(00-30365)	(00-30872)	Cello (Book & CD)	$14.95
(00-30356)	(00-30863)	Piano Accompaniment (Book & CD)	$14.95

Pop & Rock Hits
INSTRUMENTAL SOLOS

21 GUNS

ANIMAL

BOULEVARD OF BROKEN DREAMS

FIREWORK

GRENADE

HAVEN'T MET YOU YET

IN MY HEAD

JUST THE WAY YOU ARE

NEED YOU NOW

RHYTHM OF LOVE

SMILE

This book is part of a string series arranged for Violin, Viola, and Cello. The arrangements are completely compatible with each other and can be played together or as solos. Each book features a specially designed piano accompaniment that can be easily played by a teacher or intermediate piano student, as well as a carefully crafted removable part, complete with bowings, articulations and keys well suited for the Level 2-3 player. A fully orchestrated accompaniment CD is also provided. The CD includes a DEMO track of each song, which features a live string performance, followed by a PLAY-ALONG track.

This book is also part of Alfred's Pop & Rock Hits INSTRUMENTAL SOLOS series written for Flute, Clarinet, Alto Sax, Tenor Sax, Trumpet, Horn in F and Trombone. An orchestrated accompaniment CD is included. A **piano accompaniment** book (optional) is also available. Due to level considerations regarding keys and instrument ranges, the arrangements in the **wind instrument** series are not compatible with those in the **string instrument** series.

Alfred

alfred.com

Grenade - 5 - 2

Grenade - 5 - 4

JUST THE WAY YOU ARE

Words and Music by
KHALIL WALTON, PETER HERNANDEZ,
ARI LEVINE and KHARI CAIN

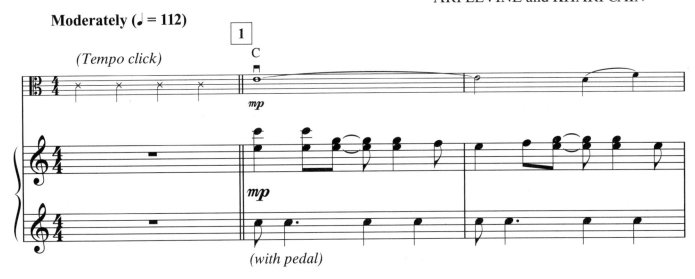

Just the Way You Are - 5 - 1

Just the Way You Are - 5 - 5

HAVEN'T MET YOU YET

Words and Music by
MICHAEL BUBLÉ, ALAN CHANG
and AMY FOSTER

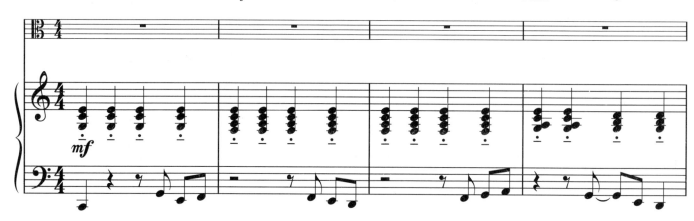

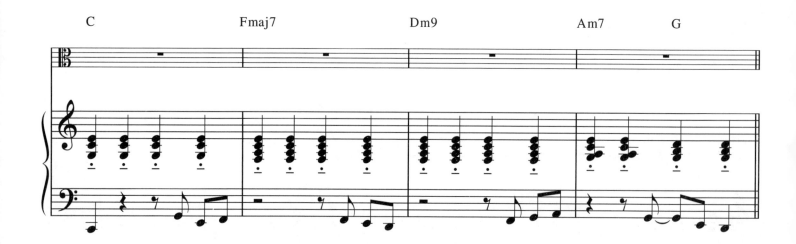

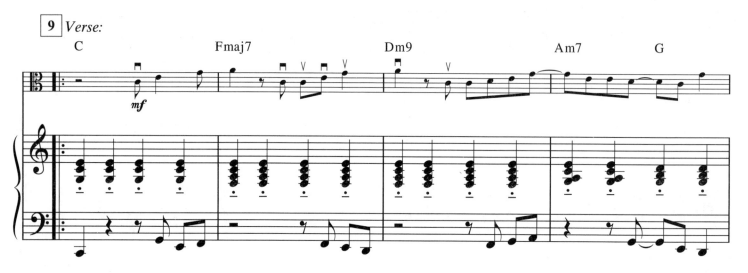

Haven't Met You Yet - 6 - 1

44

RHYTHM OF LOVE

Words and Music by
TIM LOPEZ

Rhythm of Love - 6 - 1

SMILE

Words and Music by
MATTHEW SHAFER, BLAIR DALY,
J.T. HARDING and JEREMY BOSE

Slow groove, half-time feel (♩ = 72)

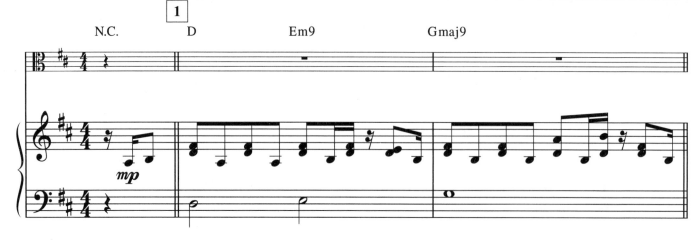

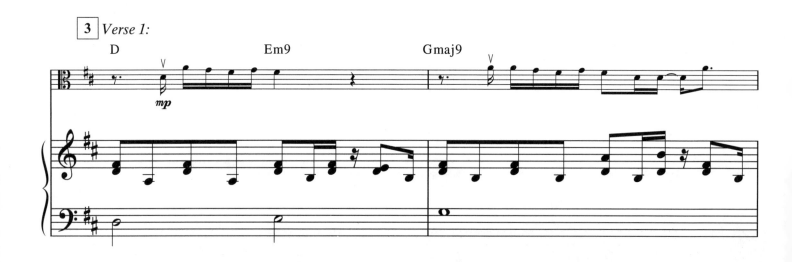

Smile - 6 - 1

56

Smile - 6 - 4

NEED YOU NOW

Words and Music by
DAVE HAYWOOD, CHARLES KELLEY,
HILLARY SCOTT and JOSH KEAR

Need You Now - 5 - 1